Poems From and Abo...
Selected by John Co...

Contents

Section 1
Dragonbirth Judith Nicholls	2
The Brave Old Duke of York Traditional	4
Queen Caroline Traditional Nursery Rhyme	4
Dandy Traditional Nursery Rhyme	5
A Poem for the Collar of the King's Dog Alexander Pope	5
Coral Christina Rossetti	6
The Mermaid Alfred Lord Tennyson	7
Who Has Seen the Wind? Christina Rossetti	8
Magpies Traditional	9
The Walk Traditional	10

Section 2
The Old Stone House Walter de la Mare	11
Questions … and Answers Wes Magee	12
Jack-in-the-Box John Mole	14
Song of the Hat Raising Doll John Mole	15
Epidaurus John Cotton	16
When I Was a Boy Charles Causley	18
Then Walter de la Mare	20
Watch's Call Traditional	21

Section 3
Winter William Shakespeare	22
The Oxen Thomas Hardy	23
Weathers Thomas Hardy	24
Hyena Anonymous	25
From **The Seafarer** Translated by John Cotton	26
Sailing Homeward Chan Fang-sheng, translated by Arthur Waley	28
Who? Charles Causley	29
Characters from **The Canterbury Tales** Geoffrey Chaucer	30
The Street Musician James Reeves	32

Edinburgh Gate
Harlow, Essex

Dragonbirth

*In the midnight mists
of long ago,
on a far-off mountainside,
there stood
a wild oak wood …*

In the wild, wet wood
there grew an oak;
beneath the oak
there slept a cave,
and in that cave
the mosses crept.

Beneath the moss
there lay a stone;
beneath the stone
there lay an egg,
and in that egg
there was a crack.

From that crack
there breathed a flame;
from that flame
there burst a fire,
and from that fire …

dragon came.

Judith Nicholls

The Rich and the Powerful

The Brave Old Duke of York

Oh, the brave old Duke of York,
He had ten thousand men,
He marched them up to the top of the hill,
And he marched them down again.
And when they were up they were up,
And when they were down they were down,
And when they were only half way up,
They were neither up nor down.

Traditional

Queen Caroline

Queen, Queen, Caroline,
Washed her hair in turpentine;
Turpentine to make it shine,
Queen, Queen, Caroline.

Traditional Nursery Rhyme

Two Dogs

Dandy

I had a dog and his name was Dandy,
His tail was long and his legs were bandy,
His eyes were brown and his coat was sandy,
The best in the world was my dog Dandy.

Traditional Nursery Rhyme

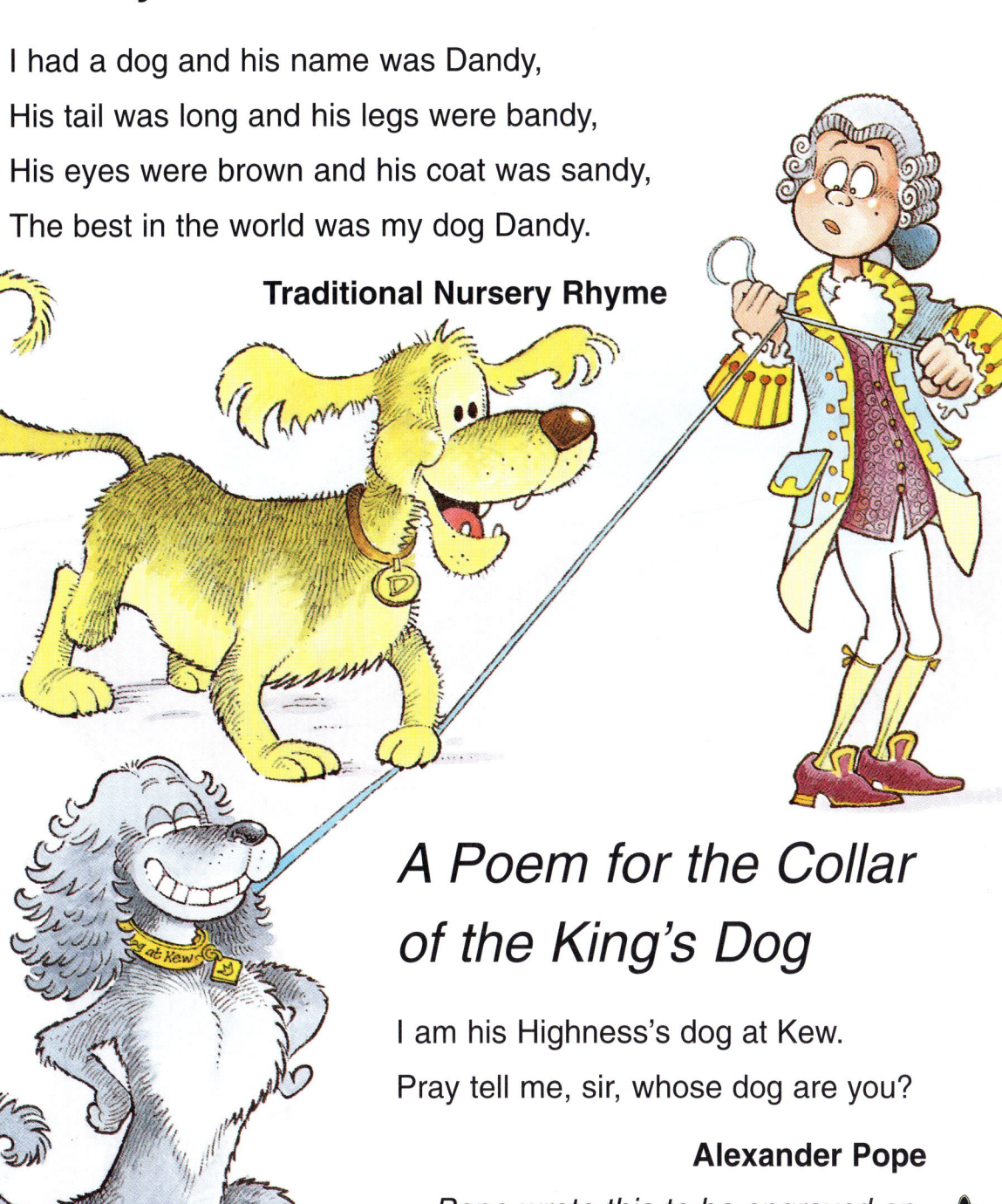

A Poem for the Collar of the King's Dog

I am his Highness's dog at Kew.
Pray tell me, sir, whose dog are you?

Alexander Pope

Pope wrote this to be engraved on the collar of King George II's dog.

Coral

O sailor, come ashore,
What have you brought for me?
Red coral, white coral,
Coral from the sea.

I did not dig it from the ground,
Nor pluck it from a tree;
Feeble insects made it
In the stormy sea.

Christina Rossetti

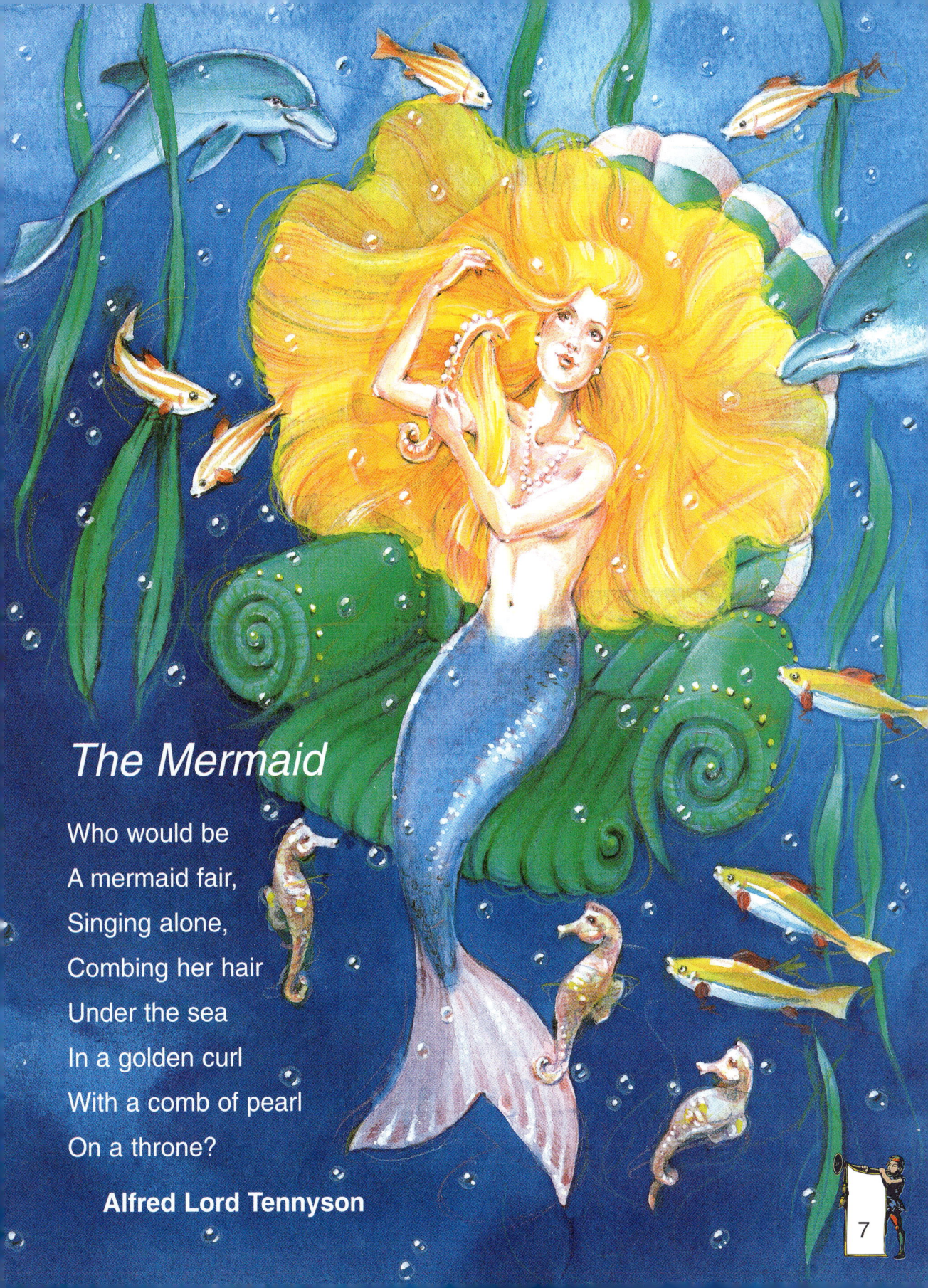

The Mermaid

Who would be
A mermaid fair,
Singing alone,
Combing her hair
Under the sea
In a golden curl
With a comb of pearl
On a throne?

Alfred Lord Tennyson

Who Has Seen the Wind?

Who has seen the wind?
Neither I nor you:
But when the leaves are trembling
The wind is passing through.

Who has seen the wind?
Neither you nor I:
But when the trees bow down their heads
The wind is passing by.

Christina Rossetti

Magpies

One for sorrow,
Two for joy,
Three for a kiss,
Four for a boy,
Five for silver,
Six for gold,
Seven for a secret
never to be told,
Eight for a letter
from over the sea,
Nine for a lover
as true as can be.

Traditional

The Walk

One day a man went for a walk.

One day a man went for a walk with his friend.

One day a man went for a walk with his friend and his dog.
The dog wore a red jacket with stripes.

One day a man went for a walk with his friend and his dog.
The dog wore a red jacket with stripes. The dog was hungry.

One day a man went for a walk with his friend and his dog.
The dog wore a red jacket with stripes. The dog was hungry
so he bit his master.

One day a man went for a walk with his friend and his dog.
The dog wore a red jacket with stripes. The dog was hungry
so he bit his master. His master got angry.

One day a man went for a walk with his friend and his dog.
The dog wore a red jacket with stripes. The dog was hungry
so he bit his master. The master got angry and he bit him back.

Traditional

The Old Stone House

Nothing on the grey roof, nothing on the brown,
Only a little greening where the rain drips down;
Nobody at the window, nobody at the door,
Only a little hollow which a foot once wore:
But still I tread on tiptoe, still tiptoe on I go,
Past nettles, porch, and weedy well, for oh, I know
A friendless face is peering, and a clear small eye
Peeps closely through the casement as my step goes by.

                              Walter de la Mare

casement – *window*

Questions ... and Answers
(A boy's version)

Where's the rattle I shook
When I was 1?

>Vanished.

Where's the Teddy I hugged
When I was 2?

>Lost.

Where's the sand-box I played in
When I was 3?

>Broken up.

Where's the beach ball I kicked
When I was 4?

>Burst.

Where's the fort I built
When I was 5?

>Destroyed.

Where's the box of comics I collected
When I was 6?

       Missing.

Where is the electric train set I loved
When I was 7?

       Given away.

Where is the holiday scrap-book I made
When I was 8?

       Disappeared.

Where is the tin of marbles I had
When I was 9?

       Swapped.

Where is the bicycle I rode
When I was 10?

       Sold.

What, all gone,
Everything?

       Yes, all gone,
       All gone ...

Wes Magee

Victorian Penny Toys

Jack-in-the-Box

Jack-in-the-Box is faithful,

Jack-in-the-Box is true

But Jack-in-the-Box

Is alone in his box

And Jack-in-the-Box wants you.

Jack-in-the-Box is cunning,

Jack-in-the-Box is sly.

Can Jack-in-the-Box

Get out of his box?

Oh Jack-in-the-Box will try.

John Mole

Song of the Hat Raising Doll

I raise my hat

And lower it.

As I unwind

I slow a bit.

This life —

I make a go of it

But tick-tock time

I know of it.

Yes, tick-tock time

I know of it.

I fear the final

O of it,

But making

A brave show of it

I raise my hat

And lower it.

John Mole

Epidaurus

The theatre at Epidaurus
Is two thousand years old,
And can seat fourteen thousand
People we're told.

It is like a great bowl
Cut out in the hills
With row upon row
Of stone seats that thrills

By its beauty, its size
And the scenery all round,
And one of its wonders
Is how any sound,

Even a whisper,
Can clearly be heard,
So those at the back
Do not miss a word.

But what thrills me most
Is all those centuries ago
Someone sat on these stones
In the very same row

That I'm sitting in now,
And across time we share
That simple excitement
Of just being there.

John Cotton

When I Was a Boy

When I was a boy
On the Isle of Wight
We all had a bath
On Friday night.
The bath was made
Of Cornish tin
And when one got out
Another got in.

First there was Jenny
Then there was Jean,
Then there was Bessie
Skinny as a bean,
Then there was Peter,
Then there was Paul,
And I was the very last
One of all.

When mammy boiled the water
We all felt blue
And we lined up like
A cinema queue.
We never had time
To bob or blush
When she went to work
With the scrubbing brush.

First there was Jenny,
Then there was Jean,
Then there was Bessie
Skinny as a bean,
Then there was Peter,
Then there was Paul,
And I was the very last
One of all.

When I was a boy
On the Isle of Wight
My Mammy went to work
Like dynamite:
Soap on the ceiling,
Water on the floor,
Mammy put the kettle on
And boil some more!

First there was Jenny,
Then there was Jean,
Then there was Bessie
Skinny as a bean,
Then there was Peter,
Then there was Paul,
And I was the very last
One of all.

Charles Causley

The Watch

The Watch was a watchman who, before there were policemen to keep the peace, used to patrol the streets of towns calling out the time and letting people know that all was well.

Then

Twenty, forty, sixty, eighty,
    A hundred years ago,
All through the night with lantern bright
    The Watch trudged to and fro,
And little boys tucked snug abed
    Would wake from dreams to hear –
'Two o' the morning by the clock,
    And the stars a-shining clear!'
Or, when across the chimney tops
    Screamed shrill a North-East gale,
A faint and shaken voice would call
    'Three! – and a storm of hail!'

Walter de la Mare

Here is another of the Watch's calls.

Watch's Call

Four of the clock

And a fine frosty morning.

Four of the clock

Sleep soundly **gentles** all.

Traditional

gentles – *a short way of saying 'gentlemen' and 'gentleladies'*

Winter

When icicles hang by the wall,
And Dick the shepherd blows his nail,
And Tom bears logs into the hall,
And milk comes frozen home in pail,
When blood is nipp'd, and ways be foul,
Then nightly sings the staring owl,
                              Tu-who;
To-whit, tu-who – a merry note.
While greasy Joan *doth keel* the pot.

When all aloud the wind doth blow.
And coughing drowns the parson's *saw*,
And birds sit brooding in the snow,
And Marian's nose looks red and raw,
When roasted crabs hiss in the bowl,
Then nightly sings the staring owl,
                              Tu-who;
Tu-whit, tu-who – a merry note,
While greasy Joan doth keel the pot.

William Shakespeare

---

doth – *does*
keel – *to cool, to prevent from boiling over*
saw – *speech or sermon*

The Oxen

Christmas Eve, and twelve of the clock.
"Now they are all on their knees,"
An elder said as we sat in a flock
By the embers in hearthside ease.

We pictured the meek mild creatures where
They dwelt in their strawy pen,
Nor did it occur to one of us there
To doubt they were kneeling then.

So fair a *fancy* few would weave
In these years! Yet, I feel,
If somebody said on Christmas Eve
"Come; see the oxen kneel,"

"In the lonely *barton* by yonder *coomb*
Our childhood used to know,"
I should go with him in the gloom,
Hoping it might be so.

Thomas Hardy

fancy – *an imaginative idea*
barton – *a farmyard*
coomb – *a small hollow or valley*

Weathers

This is the weather the cuckoo likes,
And so do I;
When showers betumble the chestnut spikes,
And nestlings fly:
And the little brown nightingale bills his best,
And they sit outside at 'The Traveller's Rest',
And the maids come forth sprig-muslin drest,
And citizens dream of the south and west,
And so do I.

This is the weather the shepherd shuns.
And so do I;
When beeches drip in browns and duns,
And thresh, and ply;
And hill-hid tides throb, throe on throe,
And meadow rivulets overflow,
And drops on gate-bars hang in a row,
And rooks in families homeward go,
And so do I.

Thomas Hardy

sprig-muslin drest – *dressed in frocks of a light cotton material decorated with patterns of small sprays of plants.*
dun – *a dull greyish brown*

Hyena

The scruffy one
who eats the meat
together with the bag
in which it is kept.
The greedy one
who eats the mother
and does not spare the child.
God's bandy-legged creature.
Killer in the night.

Anonymous

From the Yoruba, an African language, translated by Ulli Beier

From *The Seafarer*

I'll tell you the truth about myself
of travels and the hardships I've suffered,
misery endured and my experience on ships,
of countless anxieties and the fearful rolling of the waves.
Often I kept the night watch comfortless
on the ship's prow as it tossed close to the cliffs.
Harassed by cold and hunger, my feet frost bitten,
I complained of the misery that cut into my heart
and my sea-weary soul. He who gets rich on the shore
can't understand how worn out with worry
and stiff with cold I stuck out that winter,
exiled and far from my mates …
The hail flew in showers, I could hear nothing
except the pounding sea, the ice-cold waves
and, at times, the cry of the water birds.

He who lives a soft life in the city
enjoying himself, complacent and flushed with drink,
will never know what I, often dead tired,
have to put up with at sea when night darkens,
the snow comes in from the north, the deck freezes hard,
and a hoary harvest of hail begins to fall.

Translated from the Old English by John Cotton

Here is the first line of 'The Seafarer' in the original Anglo-Saxon Old English so that you can see what it looked like:

Maeg ic be me sylfum soðgied wrecan

Sailing Homeward

Cliffs that rise a thousand feet
Without a break,
Lakes that stretch a hundred miles
Without a wave,
Sands that are white through all
  the year,
Without a stain,
Pine-tree woods winter and summer
Ever green,
Streams that forever flow and flow
Without a pause,
Trees that for twenty thousand years
Your vows have kept,
You have suddenly healed the pain
  of a traveller's heart,
And moved his brush to write a
  new song.

**Chan Fang-sheng
(Fourth Century AD)
Translated by Arthur Waley**

Who?

Who is that child I see wandering, wandering?
Down by the side of the quivering stream?
Why does he seem not to hear, though I call to him?
Where does he come from, and what is his name?

Why do I see him at sunrise and sunset
Taking, in old-fashioned clothes, the same track?
Why, when he walks, does he not cast a shadow
though the sun rises and falls at his back?

Why does the dust lie so thick on the hedgerow
By the great field where a horse pulls the plough?
Why do I see only meadows, where houses
Stand in a line by the riverside now?

Why does he move like a wraith on the water,
Soft as the thistledown on the breeze blown?
When I draw near him so that I may hear him,
Why does he say that his name is my own?

Charles Causley

wraith – *ghost or apparition*

Some Characters from The Canterbury Tales

A Knight

A Knight ther was,
and that a worthy man,

That fro the tyme
that he first bigan

To ryden out,
he loved chivalrye,

Trouthe and honour,
freedom and curteiyse.

Ful worthy was he
in his lordes werre.

A Prioresse

She was so charitable and so **pitous**

She wold wepe, if that she sawe a mous

Caught in a trappe, if it were **dede or bledde**.

Of smale houndes had she, that she fedde

With rosted flesh, or milk and **wastel bred**.

The Miller

The Miller was a stout carl, for the nones,
Ful big he was of braun, and eek of bones;
That proved wel, for over-al ther he cam,
At wrastling he would have alwey the ram.
He was short-sholdred, brood and thikke knarre.

Geoffrey Chaucer

Prioresse – *a Nun in charge of a priory*
pitous – *compassionately*
dede or bledde – *dead or bleeding*
wastel bred – *finest bread*
carl – *countryman*
nones – *occasion*
braun – *muscular*
eek – *also*
the ram – *the ram, the prize*
knarre – *a thick-set fellow*

The Street Musician

(Based on the words of a song by Franz Schubert)

With plaintive fluting, sad and slow,
The old man by the roadside stands.
Who would have thought such notes could flow
From such cracked lips and withered hands?

On shivering legs he stoops and sways,
And not a passer stops to hark;
No penny cheers him as he plays;
About his feet the mongrels bark.

But piping through the bitter weather,
He lets the world go on its way.
Old piper! Let us go together,
And I will sing and you will play.

James Reeves

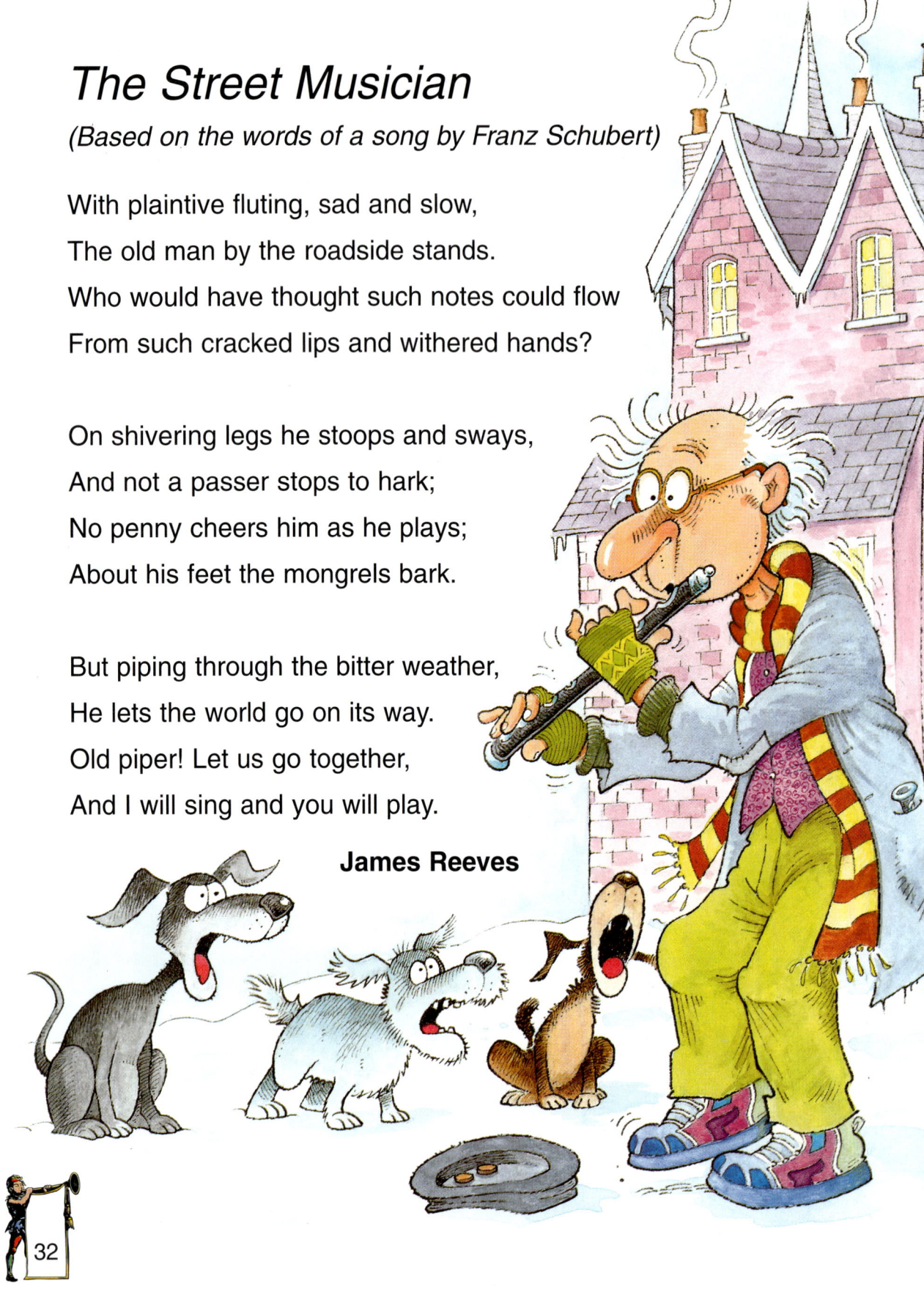